The second in a trilogy, this edition of Ashen Wanderer includes poems and ballads influenced from walking dusty trails, byways, railways and off track trekking in the night sky under the Southern Cross.

"A Journey may end yet the track always awaits you"

Dedicated to the memory of

Ronald Alexander Larcombe

13/09/1928 TO 06/02/1955

26 years

Who loved books, motorcycles & adventure

ASHEN WANDERER II

Whisper to the Breeze

Ron Hustler

Ashen Wanderer II

All inquiries and correspondence should be made to:
ashenwanderer@gmail.com

Cover Photo by Ron Hustler - Bronze sculpture by Bill Worrell, courtesy Mary Adams, owner of the Worrell Gallery. Santa Fe, New Mexico. worrellgallery.com and billworrell.com

National Library of Australia Cataloguing –in- Publication entry

Author: Hustler, Ron

Title: Ashen Wanderer : Whisper to the Breeze / Ron Hustler

ISBN: 978-0-9944523-2-0

CONTENTS

Atlas

A parched track stretches toward the horizon
Deep silhouettes greet me, lean shadows
on a harsh desert landscape.
hues of a radiant sky

Two wheels beneath me leave a
trail of lifted track, coarse humming
from the metal centaur, my Norton
howls as if charging home

Images of a fractured land and the
post war dream compete for recognition
All the while I feel free
alone in a sea of thought
Celerity wind ruffles my hair, I
lower my RAF goggles and dare to
dream as I ride the headway.

'Turning wheels take me to a
place I've never been
Burn away the miles, make me hungry,
make me lean
Bring adventure and sights unseen
for my mind to ravage on the
nomad breeze

Metal Centaur impelling on
thrust me forward to a place unknown
take me to meet my kin
then upon you I'll abscond again

I feel the desert breeze upon my face
where I've been I left no trace
where I go is unknown
no map to guide me
no direction home

Just a lonely road and a wanderlust soul
peeling the miles away as I roll
my heart pumps hard for the road ahead
and the battered tracks that I tread

Contrasting guise of the Kimberley
from the saltbush to the desert pea
behind I've left the Mallee scrub and
throttle toward the shores of Roebuck

The distance beckons as the miles toll away
riding the still of night till the sky turns to day
as the moon rises to the East
I ride hard the roaring beast
past ochre rock of rounded shapes
through eerie canyons & water napes
A distant cry through the midnight air
moves my eyes from an enduring stare

as the sun greets my back
I find a level piece of ground
where now lays my dampened swag
and dreams will orbit and ramble around'

Awaking to the rattle of passing cattle trucks
I wiped the dust from my face then set off
on my final ride to Broome
Later, sitting at the bar of the Oriental,
looking & feeling every bit the Highwayman
I toasted the long dusty trail.

'The pearling luggers work me hard
weeks at sea pass slow
but all the while the solitude
ferments my restless soul

When the boats come in
hard men sing
of pearls and daring tales
illegal deeds, intrepid needs
on the shores of Roebuck Bay

Though it is the means
when the drinking's done
to sail the coast again
and lug those pearls
from the ocean floor
up to the captain's den

Roaring out of old Broome town
on a tempest servile night
the wet season had come around
and forced me into flight
The desert road veiled me
encased me like a shroud
an unknown horizon drew me
my centaur howling proud'

Apus (Inca mountain spirits)

Our final push to the peak
saw us honour the Apus
by adding a rock 'on the pass'
atop the cairn
standing silent, gazing east
from where we came
weary miles spread out below

A shifting wind vacillates and wavers around us
we turn to the West as the sun
sets behind Nimbus clouds
attaching to the horizon
Antecedent rain
we prepare our tents for the tempest night
when dawn arrives
the sun peeks past ragged outcrops
and finds my eyes
rejoice at how the camp endured
while thoughts are set to our descent

'As the day unfurls to fading light
worn boots tramp jaded
our hearts though lift at valley's edge
with the mountain task now faded

Behind us hard days of trek
ahead us now the miles we tread
on soft meadow grass

where wildflowers spread
running streams run spritely past
spirits high, smiles cast
thin fresh air, worries least
ahead La Paz, behind us east'

Trampin' the miles aside
we discover remnants of Indigenous past
stone dwelling ruins lie amiss
artefacts undisturbed lay
maybe to the gods they pray
for descendants to return
to dwell once more
on land that now lays silent
and still
Eerie whispers proclaim sepulchre
as we quietly leave our tracks behind
compass set for bearing west
as spirits behind never rest

'Mudbrick lodgings
for wayfarers bedraggled
are a castle to a king
food and wine served upon our table
leaves us no time wasting
warmth of hearth for weary travellers
brings gratified demeanour
restful slumber and a warm sun rising
hold dreams we closely nurture'

Linn Garan

Warriors lay near Linn Garan
where the battle of Dunnichen was fought
In the province of the Picts, the northland
near the time Scotland was born

The Angles advanced up Strathmore
King Ecgfrith at the helm
a bloodthirsty Northumbrian overlord
with the Picts under his crown

At Dunnottar the Picts were sighted
the southern army flew in pursuit
then caught between the snare and Loch
the Angles met their doom

The Pictish frontier was returned
bordering the river Forth
the Northland kings were free again
befitting their gallant swords

From the sacred centre of Pictland
came the seat of the kings
"Lia Fail", the stone of Destiny
the true heart of Scotland sings

In the night sky above East Lothiam
the saltire is shining bright
and it flies blue above the northland
diagonal cross of white

Whisper

ICE
On a mountain ledge
          Precarious, belonging

LIGHT
Shining from the heavens
          Serrated, illusionary

ZENITH
Haven of loneliness
          Intrepid, amiable

OSPREY
Whispering to the breeze

Fuse

In the calm
         of my
spirit

Seeds to the
         breeze
love

plays the wind
         like an

Instrument
         of peace

Souls
         fly

they strengthen

         with
unassuming

         ease

Fate
         lies

in the distance

A measure
                    of

our means

Fuses
                burn

picking up

            speed

While Isis

            dances

at the souk

            elegant

vivid, surreal

Azure sky

            sunset

radiant, cool

Ratify

>   or recant

vexed muse

Spirits of Space

Spirits are dancing
feverishly fast
lithe forms
vividly cast

Swathing beats
movement of love
feline instinct
heart of a dove

Pensive eyes
mystic smile
tears on their cheeks
watching them cry

The ice wind blows
when the dove will shriek
tears of love
tears of this space
tears of snow
on a formless face

In spaces cold
the heart of stone
departs the soul
to traverse alone

Hawkwind

Hawkwind pretense
ardent flight
broad splashing
of art
on a canvas sky

stealthy emanation
hovering flex
predators strengths
preys vex

remaining nebulous
formless, to survive
another moment
continuous life

speed, agility
preservation reigns
fight, anticipation
stealthy sky

Intrinsic evasion
will to endure
tomorrow's sun
futures allure

Whisky Eyes

Whisky eyes for the highway
frost on the ground
deciduous leaves
nocturnal sounds

Alive in the hollows
testament to our time
travelling the byways
on tracks that we found

Whisky eyes down the highway
searching for dreams
when silence touches your soul
desire intervenes

Tramped for nights
on the eastern ridge
saw quolls & southern boobooks
in the dark chill pitch

Whisky eyes alight to the moon
as the pitta bird flies
not a night too soon
Northward bound in the night
heading home with a guiding light

Walking the wilds of time
hear my nocturnal cries
walking the wilds of time
serenaded by whisky eyes

Rainshadow

Striding
an exit
Mojave Desert night
stretching across basin and range
                              spirit
Mojave tribe
                    lives...

Joshua trees
scattered
Tehachapi Mountain Range
San Andreas
                    fault
rainshadow shaman
                    came...

Pacific Northwest
storm
Cajun pass
winds
desert star trampin'

                    west
searching for
                    kin...

Bohemian
wanderer
mind aglow
doors of

perception

shimmering

stone...

Full moon
risin'
desert pyre
vale, Mojave

soul

desert

fire...

Fires

I wish to be eternal
for my soul desires
not boundaries
but infinite fires

Sacred ancient land

We dropped our packs
on the battery track
then took a bearing
to the bluff
out for days near the Spencer Gulf
trampin' rough

Seven kin on a lonely trail
north east to Fricks Dam
where a night was spent
in the Mallee scrub
where the ring neck parrots band

We trekked a spur to cliffs edge
and screed a steep decent
found ripples of ancient creek bed
Gondwanaland it's said

Heading south, remnants
of an age old tribal bowl
bore of rock beside a spring
living, ancient soul

Past Red Cliffs
down to Hidden Creek
then up to Hidden Gorge
the seven trekked

forged a path
that left no trace in course

That night I heard
an ancient soul
walk on through our camp
then as the moon rose
through the sky
I tramped the spur alone

While others slept below
a presence swept around
spirits of an ancient past
connected to this land
though fear I gripped
I kept tight lipped
and tried to understand
but ancient is
what ancient was
this time it took a stand
it beat me down
from that spur
down to the lower land
away from it's sacred place
sacred ancient land

Flinders Ranges

Red, sandy
stretching west
sparse green plains
eyes following the track
for miles
escaping threatening rains

Navigating Melrose topographic
up to Wild Dog Creek
through Murray Town
along Dustbowl Road
shadowed by Mt Remarkable peak

Knolls are many and creeks
flow through
between the weaving spurs
trekkers will find their way
to the distant range
unperturbed

Away from road trains
that ply their trade
on the busy highway near
away from the ports
that line the gulf
away, your mind will clear

Up into the ranges
with your pack
your trampin' boots
where the emus
and the Yellowfoot
traverse the gnarly roots

The rocky ground
and dry creek beds
where wildflowers abound
Cassinia Laevis, Mallee scrub
in deep red gorges found

Pinnacles and caves
hold dreamtime spirits
close
the message in the wind
you hear
is for wise men under oath

When the storm clouds gather
from the west
to meet the winter range
ancient voices gather
on the breeze
and whisper from their naves
along the ridges and deep valley creeks

the sound is all the same
they let you pass, with respect
to weave through
their ancient domain

RAL 6/2/55

Stationed at Coonawarra, 1954
on the navy wireless
Protecting our northern shore
at HMAS Melville
I lay down my worn swag
packed away my gear
stowed my duffle bag

I worked communications
toiled away my shifts
mind intently focused
on static electronic drifts

Had been travelling for sometime
through NSW towns
from my birthplace of Goulburn
worked on the railways of the crown

Rode my bikes with pride
English roaring beasts
down dusty tracks
through the west
then over to the east

Held my head high
Scottish pride within
I blew my father's bagpipes
and rolled from his tobacco tin,
Drank whisky at the Gordon
amongst the smoky din
trapped rabbits up on Turners farm
then took them home to skin

Celebrated oft in Darwin
to draw the heat away
but ended up on charge
with my captain holding sway

As the year came to a close
seventy pounds bought my bike
A 1949 Matchless
G3L, did it have bite

I stripped it down
then rebuilt,
had her purring loud
I rode her around
Darwin town
strong, lean and proud

In '55 we throttled south
past Howard Springs,
into a four dog night
over rugged tracks

under the stars
roaring with all our might

The day next came
I lay adrift
too far from my home
the roaring beast just
flew too fast
and sent me on alone
with the setting sun
to the west
my spirit on the breeze
as my thoughts returned
to Joshua Street
to be with family.

For Hazel, Jack, Margaret & Ivor

Southern Ocean sojourn

I was treading on the edge of the moon

travelling through the night

feeling, well like a natures child

free, energised, high

time passed in my peripheral

I noticed ice

cracking, like thunder

the breeze was sombre

music drifted by in fractured notes

quavers, not jazz, then silence

I was still, leaning into the glistening thread

anticipating

eyes closed, my hair blowing slightly

the distance was closing in

circular horizons

rings of mystery

forming lips to kiss me

and make me cry

Retreating to shelter

I lay

embryonic, on granite

balancing beside gravity

praying

for a vision

that will guard my dreams

protect my soul

smile on my being

I saw love

I saw eternity

Cenizo arrante

Hearts resonate
upon stars aloft
lucid, pure
warmth's reflect
radiant and true
sense
loves connect

Ascending to the rim
of a pale moon
stars fall into our palms
anjali mudra
spiritual lotus
our hearts
our calm
shine on

Southern Ocean reprise

Farewell,
ode to the Southern Ocean
as dreams sail by
Angels watch
their hearts open
Pulsating
upon crest and trough
awaiting
the sailors cry

Tumult and passion
clashing
of sea and mind
white peaks
frisk and frolic
in uncertain time
Pensive thoughts
wide and vast
upon a plateau of ice
that drifts
robust, fragile

From unknown depths
Mammal of Fate
breaches
Mercurial moment

Silence filled tension
Earth and Moon and Sun
Calm crossed the oceans
touching everyone

Yet the ocean boiled
in stormy tempest
(Harpoons crossed the bow)
Then the warriors bore
on every wave crest
Hearts, beating gently
by their side, angels
Love being sentry
in the aftermath to come
Planet Blue Om

Wintry haven

Oh wintry haven
deep coastal pools
of blue
rigid granite outcrops
overlooking white capped seas

Oh wintry haven
embrace me
unfurl your secrets
and whispers
upon the wind
let them reach
the overlooking sky

Bear upon the land
your magic runes
sweep up the autumn
penchant
A longing come too soon
Oh wintry Haven............

Edeowie

Gap to the pound
up Wilpena way
where desert stars shine
whilst thirst is your bane

Following late afternoon skies
the fellowship forged ahead
through rain and hail
then at Cooinda slept

With the eastern glow rising
known waterhole dry
Malloga Falls whispers
where the wedge-tails fly

Entering the gorge
with a pack haul and climb
boulder hopped down
the trek lead mine

Admiring the wonder and beauty
of a place so harsh
holding trees and stones
where few will pass

Leaves are whistling
in fore, of steep gorge walls
red hues, blue skies
a backdrop to pause

Sound of the eagle
above, out of sight
cries of its prey
caught in claws of might

And so we pass
holding in awe
sights we view
sights we saw

We descend the cliff
at Glenora Falls
then scramble to a ledge
a hundred metres tall

As we peer down
to the rocks below
we haul along
our packs in tow
a light shower wets
the ledge ahead
focus intense
or pray instead

Clambering down
in late afternoon
slow trampin' between
the last falls too
another climb around
the falls edge
with our backs exposed
to nothing but air
screeing to the base
of Kanalla Falls
setting up camp
amongst desert gums tall

Then so we sleep
with calm ambience
on the waxing moon
in the womb of our tents

Next day's water taken
from the base of the falls
then maps in our hands
we take up the cause
saddle of Mt Abrupt
without a pause

Climbing the range
from west to east
ten hours ahead
a tramping feast

crossing creeks
to the north
the sight we seek
is the saddle adjacent
to Mt Abrupt peak

When at last
it comes to view
we climb the spur
with added vigour
traverse around
to meet the creek
to stand atop
looking east

To the valley below
we make our descent
throats dry, alert
intrepid thoughts vent

Nodding my head
in a sign of respect
to this dry desert landscape
whose secret is kept
by those who wander
who perish of thirst
who become the spirits
and the deserts lament

Flinders

Bone
dry
rocks lay desolate
ground of pyre

Scattered
are the creatures
who wandered
scattered
are the souls dispersed

Parched
alive.........sighing
in this landscape

Harshness
evolves
into wild........thirst

Full moon
shines
dry throats
reach
(for hope)

Thoughts
touch the ground
where
spirits lie

Life
rains fall
spirits rise
ascending
on sunbeams
to the shepherd's
call

Dark etchings (shadows lament)

Shadows grow behind a
midnight pew
as the night lays down
a waxing moon
shaping, wavering on the
night born breeze
darkness etching a placid
release

Existing not to be in vain
with moments bruised
in times refrain
nature sows a wild heave
on rocks, on ochre
on the breeze

Following, weaving in the
silent shrill
winds rescind, to leave a still
when darkness breaks on
the dawning day
we forge a change at the
suns first ray

Peruse, thy eternal view
laid down by sun
laid down by moon
mimicked shape in a backlit
snare
impassive plethora of grey
laid bare

Hoja

Falling
caressing the breeze
grace in pendulum
gravitational drift

Shaped
by rustic hue
silent veins
protrude
to land
as by chance
meeting
autumn's mood

Droplet

Droplet

spherical, glistening

transparent

in the autumn sun

Grampians (southern star)

Time began as Bunjil
created Gariwerd
he flew as Werpil to survey
his creation
when his time arrived
he rose above the land
a star of the dreamtime

As the Southern Cross watched
from an ancient sky

Jardwadjali man drank
from his kangaroo pouch water bag
the sixth season was bullambar
butterflies filled the sky
Gamadj, his totem, flew above
yellow tail, shrieking cry

While the Southern Cross watched
from an ancient sky

And all the while
white cockatoos fly
above the sandstone ridges
stony creeks and forest plains

as the Southern Cross watched
from an ancient sky

In the season of bullambar
when butterflies filled the sky
Ashen Wanderer trekked the paths
where Jardwadjali man now flies
spirits on the totem breeze
surveying the land below

And all the while the Southern Cross
watched from an ancient sky

Grampians Girrawheen (place of flowers)

To the mountains
with wandering aim
a night sky radiance
eyes in flame

Catching dreams
of spirits that fly
around rock faces
and Mundaring
in the mid of night

Holding their meaning
their reason
for a moment of dreaming
spirits that dwell
both connected and free
on the sacred land
of the sacred tree

Ridges and spurs murmur
in darkness and chill
voices of old
searching
the void to fill

Bunjil wings
of mountain and being
animus connection
unseen
heed the song
timelines beneath
to the land
I bequeath
all of my wandering
my entire stream
as spirits flow
on the ashen breeze
your earth
to stand or fly
hark
for the requiem cry

Wild spirit (leaf)

Leaf wild spirit
fly
open the sky
distance and time
levitate
until gravity
you
no longer defy

Drifting by
leaf wild spirit
fly
open the sky
drift by

Wild spirit (star)

Open
your palm
star rising

Touch the sky
settle

Echoes of light
shine
illuminate strength
wisdom
eternity
shine on

Cowries – Feathers – Stone

The peace that gathers
upon the shore
where cowries lay washed
from the ocean floor
wandering along, to collect
romantic gesture
that will affect
ripen the soul that lays before
silent-still
beyond my door

the feathers that waft down
laying gentle
upon the ground
where paths and tracks
are left behind
my feet will lightly tramp
then for *Satpursha* I will find
from birds
of many different kinds
patterns-colours
which find their way
into her heart
every day

As the sacred stones lay
along Gap Point
upon the wind
truth holds sway
while above glide
birds of prey
droplets reach towards the shore
to round the stones
smooth once more
holding in my palm – a peace
serene-calm

Wall

Paint the wall
black
superimpose
a track

In the sky a crack
to let the light in

Ride my centaur
into the wall

Dreams to explore
cracks to let the light
fall

on my wall
on my wall

Tsankawi

On this land
 I seek
Tewa Pueblo spirits
Whispering

On this land
they speak
to those
who walk alone

On this land
the raven stares
through time

Guide me through your
desert lands
spirit masters of
all man

On this land
of timeless
Dust and thunder

Ronald Alexander Larcombe

The destination is not of import
embark
the journey becomes the event.

Ronald Alexander Larcombe

Ivor Larcombe

www.ingramcontent.com/pod-product-compliance
Lightning Source LLC
Chambersburg PA
CBHW071733020426
42331CB00008B/2007